Great Moments in Canadian Baseball

BRIAN KENDALL

LESTER PUBLISHING

Canadian Cataloguing in Publication Data

Kendall, Brian
    Great moments in Canadian baseball

Includes index.
ISBN 1-895555-55-8

1. Baseball – Canada – History.   I. Title.

GV863.15.A1K46   1995   796.357'0971   C95-930154-2

Lester Publishing Limited
56 The Esplanade
Toronto, Ontario
Canada M5E 1A7

Printed and bound in Canada

95 96 97 98   5 4 3 2 1

For Phil and Irene Marchildon

Contents

Introduction

Babe, Yankee Clipper, Georgia Peach. Most Canadian baseball fans know these famous nicknames belong to immortals called Ruth, DiMaggio, and Cobb. But how many can link the handles Tip, Mooney, and Penetang Phil with James O'Neill, George Gibson, and Phil Marchildon, three of the greatest ballplayers this country has ever produced?

Too often Canadians, unaware of our long and proud baseball heritage, have bought into the belief that the game is a wholly American invention. In fact, baseball has been played in Canada since at least 1838, a full year before Abner Doubleday's mythical invention of the sport in Cooperstown, New York. There is documented proof that on June 4 of that year, an early variation of the game was played in the hamlet of Beachville, Ontario, out on a smooth pasture near the present-day Baptist church.

By the 1860s teams and leagues were being formed throughout Canada. The first Canadian-born major leaguer was Bill Phillips, a first baseman from Saint John, New Brunswick, who broke in with Cleveland of the National League in 1879. Since then, more than 180 native sons have worn big-league uniforms. The shining moments of the best of them are fondly recalled on these pages, but there are still others whose stories should not be forgotten.

One is Toronto's Arthur "Foxy" Irwin, a slick-fielding shortstop often credited with inventing the baseball glove. In 1883, after breaking two fingers on his left hand while playing for the National League's Providence Grays, Irwin called on a "glover" to help him adapt an oversized buckskin driving glove by padding it, making a fastening at the back, and leaving room for his bandages. Within two years, almost every professional was wearing what was called the "Irwin glove."

Later on came Jack Graney of St. Thomas, Ontario, an outstanding defensive outfielder with the Cleveland Indians from 1908 to 1922. Graney was the first major leaguer to face a rookie left-handed pitcher named Babe Ruth, rapping a single to left field. He was also the first to wear a number on his uniform and was the first athlete to move to the broadcast booth after his playing days were over, serving for many years as the Indians' play-by-play man.

Another innovator was Russell "Doctor" Ford of Brandon, Manitoba, who had the dubious distinction of having invented the emery-board pitch back in the days when such trick deliveries were not considered illegal. By scuffing the ball with a piece of emery paper hidden in a hole in his glove, Ford was able to win a phenomenal twenty-six games as a rookie with the New York Yankees in 1910.

Other memorable Canadian-born players include George Selkirk of Huntsville, Ontario, who starred with the Yankees from 1934 to 1942, and Jeff Heath, a big, powerful outfielder from Fort William, Ontario, who slugged 194 homers while playing with four different teams between 1936 and 1949. But both Selkirk and Heath grew up in the United States, where they first learned to play the game and where they lived out their lives.

The career highlights of such born-and-bred Canadians as Goody Rosen, Ron Taylor, Ferguson Jenkins, and Larry Walker are recounted here. Also remembered are those ballplayers who came to this country and left their mark: a young Babe Ruth, Jackie Robinson, and so many unforgettable members of the Montreal Expos and Toronto Blue Jays.

Great Moments in Canadian Baseball salutes their achievements—and celebrates a game Canadians have played, and often excelled at, since that first recorded gathering in a Beachville pasture back in 1838.

Tip O'Neill breaks hearts and bats .492

It's said that every time tall and handsome James "Tip" O'Neill came to bat for the St. Louis Browns, a dozen women wearing flowing robes would rise from the crowd and sound a fanfare on silver trumpets. Canada's first baseball hero was so adored by his public that hundreds of children were named after him, including the Tip O'Neill who would one day gain fame as U.S. Speaker of the House.

The son of a Woodstock, Ontario, innkeeper, O'Neill was introduced to baseball when a guest showed him how to throw a curve ball. In 1883 he became the first Canadian to pitch in the major leagues, but it was as a batsman that O'Neill rose to prominence. By 1885 he was a hitting star and full-time outfielder for the St. Louis Browns, the dominant team of the American Association, which at the time was considered a major league and played in a postseason World Series against the National League.

O'Neill compiled a remarkable .492 average during the 1887 campaign, the highest in the history of the game. Even subtracting the bases on balls (which for that one season were counted as hits), his average still works out to .435, second only to the .438 hit by Hugh Duffy of the Boston Nationals in 1894.

"He was not a fly hitter . . . O'Neill drove them on a line," Lou Schlier, the Browns' mascot, recalled many years later. Pitchers would turn their backs in fear after delivering the ball to him.

O'Neill—who earned the nickname "Tip" for his ability to foul-tip balls and work pitchers for walks—gave notice of what was to come early in the 1887 campaign when, on two occasions, he hit for the cycle, with a single, double, triple, and home run in the same game. By the end of the regular schedule on October 9, O'Neill led the majors in hits (225), doubles (52), triples (19), and home runs (14).

He topped his league in batting again the next year and compiled a career average of .326 over ten seasons. When his playing days were over, Canada's greatest hitter ran a saloon in Montreal. He died on New Year's Eve, 1915, and was buried in Woodstock.

ST. LOUIS BALL CLUB, 1888.
American Association Champions, 1888.

O'Neill's St. Louis Browns were the dominant team of the era, winning four straight American Association pennants and two World Series titles between 1885 and 1888. O'Neill is pictured at the top left of the second row.

Opposite:
Remembered back home as the Woodstock Wonder, O'Neill compiled a .326 batting average over ten years and is the only Canadian to record two hundred hits in a season.

Mooney Gibson puts the brakes on Ty Cobb

Before the start of the World Series between Pittsburgh and Detroit, there was a lot of loose talk about how Ty Cobb would run wild on Pirates catcher George "Mooney" Gibson. During the regular season, the Tiger star had terrorized the American League by stealing a record seventy-six bases. Although Gibson, who had learned his baseball on the sandlots of London, Ontario, was known to possess a powerful and accurate throwing arm, the consensus was that

One of the game's greatest defensive catchers, Gibson was at his best in 1909, leading his league in fielding average and putouts, and batting a career-high .265.

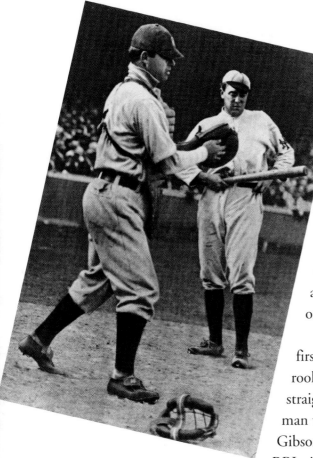

Gibson, the last Canadian to manage in the major leagues, guided the Pirates and Chicago Cubs when his playing days were over. He was fired after leading Pittsburgh to consecutive second-place finishes in 1932 and 1933.

no backstop alive could stop the great Tyrus.

When the Series was all over on October 16, however, the Pirates had edged the Tigers four games to three and Gibson's brilliance behind the plate was heralded as one of the decisive factors in Pittsburgh's victory.

He had held Cobb to just two steals, one in each of the first two contests. He was also masterful in his handling of rookie pitcher Charles "Babe" Adams, who won three straight games for the Pirates. And, uncharacteristically for a man who would hit just .236 over fourteen big-league seasons, Gibson had helped out with his bat, stroking six hits with two RBIs, including the winning run in the Series opener.

Gibson had become such a hero to his home-town fans since breaking in with the Pirates in 1905 that trainloads of Londoners made the trip across the border for the four games in Detroit. His followers "were equipped with horns, rattles and other noise-making devices and used them," reported the *London Advertiser.* "Shouts of 'Oh, you, Gibson' greeted the Pittsburgh star."

Following the Pirates' victory, Gibson was fêted at a civic reception back in London. His train was met by a horde of well-wishers who carried him from the platform. The procession of automobiles, dignitaries, and bands then slowly made its way to Victoria Park, where five thousand people thronged around a small stage.

"I want to thank you for this reception," said Gibson, who during a long career as a player, coach, and manager would come home to London every off-season. "In years to come I can look back on tonight as one of the happiest of my life.

"And may I say," he concluded, "I shall always be a Canadian." 11

The Babe goes deep for the first time

A big, unsophisticated, pleasure-loving kid who could hardly believe his good fortune in being able to play baseball for a living, George Herman Ruth was just nineteen when his International League Providence Grays arrived in Toronto to play the local Maple Leafs. Ruth had spent most of his life to that point confined in a Baltimore school for incorrigible boys.

People had started to call him Babe earlier in the season soon after Jack Dunn, the owner of the minor-league Baltimore Orioles, signed the left-handed pitcher to his first professional contract.

"Dunn practically led me by the hand from the dressing room to the pitcher's box," Ruth recalled. "I was as proud of my Orioles' uniform as I had been of my first long pants . . . 'Look at Dunnie and his new babe,' one of the older players yelled. That started it."

Since then, Ruth had been sold to the Boston Red Sox, where he had ten impressive innings of major-league work before being sent down to the Sox farm club in Providence to help out in their fight for the International League pennant.

In the contest against the Maple Leafs, who played their home games at eighteen-thousand-seat Hanlan's Point Stadium on the Toronto Islands, Ruth demonstrated the pitching ability that would soon make him the top southpaw in the American League, as well as the raw power at the plate that would revolutionize the sport.

In the sixth inning the Babe smashed a pitch from Toronto pitcher Ellis Johnson over the fence in right field for his first professional home run — the only one he would ever hit in the minor leagues. Ruth also pitched his best game of the season that Saturday afternoon, surrendering only one hit in a 9–0 shutout.

The next day the headline in *The Globe*, a local daily, read: "Leafs Couldn't Get Runner Past First; Only One Hit Made Off Pitcher Babe Ruth."

In 1985 Toronto mayor Art Eggleton declared Hanlan's Point an historic site. A commemorative plaque was placed where the baseball stadium once stood — and where the young Babe Ruth began to make history.

A nineteen-year-old Babe Ruth is seen here in the uniform of the Providence Grays, the Boston Red Sox farm club in the International League.

Opposite:
History's greatest slugger broke into the professional ranks as a pitcher. Ruth won eighteen games in 1915 for Boston, then had twenty-three- and twenty-four-win seasons before turning his attention to swinging for the fences.

Dick Fowler no-hits the Browns

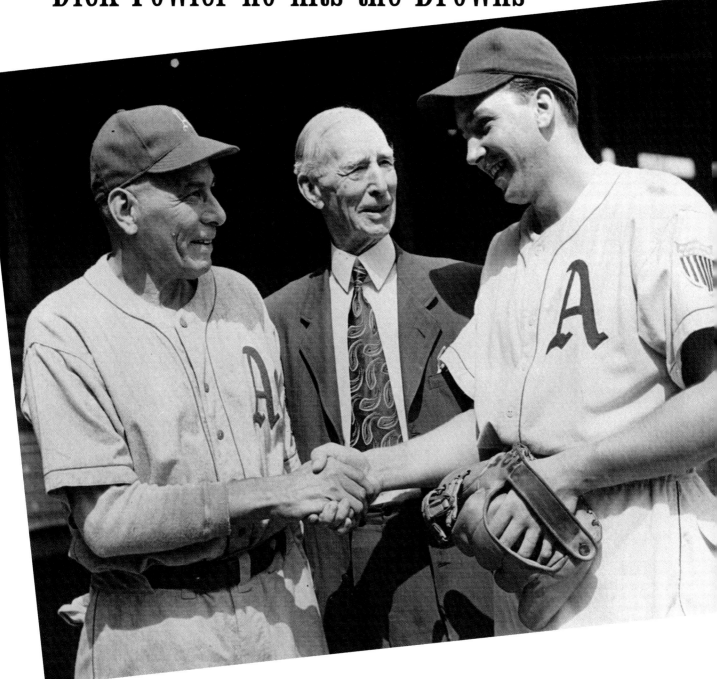

"I'm a pretty lucky guy, I guess," a stunned Dick Fowler kept repeating to reporters after he became the only Canadian ever to toss a major-league no-hitter.

The 6-foot-4, twenty-four-year-old right-hander had only recently returned to Connie Mack's Philadelphia Athletics after serving more than thirty months

Dick Fowler accepts the congratulations of Chief Bender, who had himself pitched a no-hitter for the Athletics in 1910. Standing between them is the legendary Connie Mack, owner and manager of the American League team.

The no-hitter came in Fowler's first start since his return from wartime duty in the Canadian Army. He and fellow Canadian Phil Marchildon would anchor Philadelphia's starting staff for the next several years.

as a private in the Canadian Army. His 1–0 whitewash of the St. Louis Browns at Philadelphia's Shibe Park was his first starting assignment since 1942.

Fowler, who was born in Toronto and played juvenile baseball in local Kiwanis leagues before turning professional at seventeen, walked four men, but two were erased with double plays. The Browns were able to send only five balls farther than the Athletics' infield.

Buddy Rosar, the A's catcher, said Fowler had tied the Browns in knots with a fine curve ball, a change of pace, and a fastball that was unusually "alive." Rosar added that "mixed with this was a combination half fork and slider. I wouldn't have got a good foul if I had been batting against him."

The 16,755 fans in attendance became aware of the possibility of a no-hit game as early as the fifth inning. From that point on, they cheered every time St. Louis made an out. The situation was made even more tense by the fact that Browns pitcher John Miller was also throwing shut-out ball.

Finally, in the bottom of the ninth, the scoreless deadlock was broken when Philadelphia's Hal Peck tripled to the left-field fence and then scored on a single to centre by Irv Hall.

Immediately after the winning run crossed the plate, Fowler ran out to shake hands with Miller, who had allowed only five hits. He was then swept up onto the shoulders of the screaming crowd and paraded around the infield.

Still in a state of shock, Fowler confessed that there was no way he could have continued to pitch if the A's had failed to score in the ninth. Overweight and out of shape from his time away from the game, Fowler said he was ready to collapse from exhaustion.

"I can honestly say I was never in worse shape in my life," admitted the young Torontonian, who would win sixty-six games during a ten-year career. "I have no explanation for the no-hitter. It just happened."

15

Goody Rosen gets even

Toronto's Goody Rosen felt he'd never been treated fairly or with the proper respect by the Brooklyn Dodgers. That made his payback all the sweeter when it finally came.

Known as the "Toronto Tidbit" because he stood 5-foot-9 and weighed just 155 pounds, Rosen broke in with the Dodgers in 1937. While playing full-time the next season, he hit .281 and was the outstanding defensive outfielder in the National League, with a fielding average of .989.

But early in 1939, Rosen injured his leg sliding into first. Though the doctors told him to rest, Leo Durocher, the Dodgers' famously hard-nosed manager, insisted he keep playing. When Rosen's average plunged, Durocher banished him to Brooklyn's minor-league farm club in Montreal.

It was another five years before Rosen made it back to the big leagues. In May 1944 the Dodgers traded two players to Syracuse of the International League to reacquire his rights. Rosen thought hard about telling Durocher to take his job and shove it, but he knew that at age thirty-two, this would be his last chance.

The cigar-smoking, wisecracking little outfielder became the darling of the Brooklyn fans the next season when he batted .325, third best in the National League. He was named an all-star and there was even a special day held in his honour at Ebbets Field.

Naturally, Rosen figured he had earned a sizeable raise in pay — but he was in for another disappointment. Brooklyn president Branch Rickey told him that with younger outfielders returning from the war, Rosen was now expendable. Rickey sold him to Brooklyn's crosstown rivals, the New York Giants, on April 27.

Rosen took out all his disgust and pent-up anger the very next day when, as fate would have it, Brooklyn played a doubleheader at the Polo Grounds, home field of the Giants.

Rosen addresses the crowd during a special day held in his honour at Brooklyn's Ebbets Field during the 1945 season. That year he hit .325, but missed his chance to play in the All-Star Game when it was cancelled because of wartime travel restrictions.

Following his trade to the Giants in 1946, Rosen batted .281 in one hundred games. He was sent back to the minors in September after injuring his arm in an outfield crash.

In front of a crowd of more than fifty-six thousand, Rosen enjoyed the greatest day of his career, collecting five hits, including a three-run homer, as the Giants swept both games. The twin losses would prove critical to Brooklyn, who ended the season in a tie with the Cardinals for first place. St. Louis then beat the Dodgers in a playoff to advance to the World Series.

If Durocher and Rickey hadn't been in such a hurry to trade Rosen, if they'd waited even one day, Brooklyn might have taken at least one of the two games in that fateful doubleheader and won the pennant.

The revenge of the Toronto Tidbit was complete.

17

Jackie Robinson finds a northern home

Jackie Robinson had been under almost unbearable pressure since signing an historic contract with the Brooklyn Dodgers' Montreal farm team in the fall of 1945.

As the first black since the last century to play what was called organized baseball, Robinson was met with unmasked hatred throughout the cities of the International League. In Baltimore, the circuit's southernmost city, he wasn't allowed to stay in the same hotel as his teammates. Angry crowds constantly jeered him and opposing players charged into him at second base with spikes aimed high.

But in Montreal—a city Brooklyn boss Branch Rickey chose because of its reputation for racial tolerance—Robinson found a safe haven. From the start the fans had taken him to their hearts and made him welcome.

"I felt a jubilant sense of gratitude for the way the Canadians expressed their feelings," Robinson later wrote. "The people of Montreal were warm and wonderful."

The marvellously gifted twenty-seven-year-old responded with a brilliant campaign, topping the league with a .349 batting average while leading the Royals to the International League pennant and a spot in the Little World Series against Louisville.

When Robinson's clutch hitting and his daring on the basepaths sparked the Royals to a comeback victory in the series, the joyous fans loudly showed their love, refusing to leave Montreal Stadium until Robinson returned for one last bow. By now they and all of baseball knew that his stay in their city was over, that Robinson's next task would be to break the colour barrier in the major leagues.

The crowd stormed around him when he finally returned to the field wearing street clothes, almost ripping the shirt from his back. Then they chased him through the streets of Montreal. As a black journalist would write, "It was probably the only day in history that a black man ran from a white mob with love instead of lynching on his mind."

In his one season with the Royals, Robinson batted a league-leading .349 and sparked Montreal's drive to the 1946 Little World Series.

**Opposite:
Despite the objections of every other team in the majors, Brooklyn boss Branch Rickey courageously signed Robinson to play for the Dodgers in 1947.**

18

Bombers downed by Marchildon on Opening Day

It was the game that signalled thirty-three-year-old Phil Marchildon's recovery from the horrors of his wartime duty—and that marked the start of one of the greatest seasons any Canadian pitcher has ever had.

"There wasn't a moment when I didn't feel I was in complete control," the Philadelphia Athletics' ace said of his six-hit, 6–1 victory over the mighty Bronx Bombers. His performance at Yankee Stadium came in front of an Opening Day crowd of 39,344 that included ex-president Herbert Hoover. "My fastball and curve hummed and snapped, and the Yankee hitters were baffled by a new forkball I'd unveiled for the first time."

The war had forced the native of Penetanguishene, Ontario, to interrupt a brilliant career that saw him win ten games as a rookie in 1941. The next season Marchildon emerged as one of the game's newest pitching stars when he posted a 17–14 record for a last-place Athletics' squad.

Then he enlisted as a tail gunner in the Royal Canadian Air Force. On his twenty-sixth mission Marchildon's plane was shot into the sea off Denmark. He spent the rest of the war in Stalag Luft III, the prison camp that was the scene of the Great Escape, and on the infamous Death March, when the Germans herded thousands of cold and hungry POWs through the ruins of the Reich to prevent Allied troops from liberating them.

Though he was sick with dysentery and his nerves were frayed almost to the breaking point from his ordeal, Marchildon fought back to win thirteen games in 1946. His dominating performance

Called Penetang Phil after his home town of Penetanguishene, Ontario, Marchildon didn't turn professional until the age of twenty-five. But less than two years later, he was starring for Connie Mack's Philadelphia Athletics. The right-hander would win sixty-eight games over nine seasons.

Marchildon demonstrates his lethal new forkball for the press following his Opening Day victory.

the following Opening Day in New York served notice that he was fully recovered and was pitching better than ever.

"With a few breaks I might be able to hit that twenty-win mark," a confident Marchildon told the press. By season's end the right-hander's 19–9 record fell just short of his goal, but many in baseball had come to regard him as the premier hurler in the American League.

"When I was at the top of my game I felt I could beat anyone," Marchildon said years later. "That day in New York— and right through that entire season—I was as good as I could possibly be."

A tail gunner on a Halifax bomber during the war, Marchildon was shot down on his twenty-sixth mission. He was interned in Stalag Luft III, the notorious German prison camp that was the scene of the Great Escape.

Rookie Pete Ward sparks the White Sox

Smash debuts were becoming something of a specialty for twenty-four-year-old Pete Ward. As a late-season call-up with the Baltimore Orioles in 1962, he had stroked a two-run, pinch-hit single in his first major-league at bat to defeat the Minnesota Twins and prevent Camilo Pascual's twentieth victory.

Now, following an off-season trade to the Chicago White Sox, Ward was the team's starting third baseman as they opened the season in Detroit. The Tigers were leading 5–4 when Ward came to the plate in the seventh and deposited a Jim Bunning offering into the right-field grandstand. The three-run homer, the first of twenty-two in what would be a spectacular

Pete Ward led the White Sox in most offensive categories during his brilliant rookie season. He finished second to Carl Yastrzemski for most hits in the American League and was runner-up to Dick Stuart for total bases.

22

rookie season, provided the edge as Chicago won 7–5.

"I've always hit wherever I've been," the cocky Ward told reporters, "so I can't see any reason why I shouldn't hit here."

Born in Montreal, where his father, Jim, played with the National Hockey League's Maroons and Canadiens, Ward was a singles hitter who was gripping the bat with his hands held six inches apart when he turned professional in 1958. Once the Orioles convinced him to close his grip, Ward began to hit with power, although his batting style remained one of the most unorthodox in baseball. While in a deep crouch, the left-handed hitter would point his rear foot straight at the plate, with his front foot directed at the pitcher. "I've got a real silly stance," Ward admitted. "Fundamentally, I've got a bad swing."

Nonetheless, he followed his Opening Day heroics by hitting safely in eighteen consecutive games, the longest hitting streak of the year in the American League. By the end of the season, he led the White Sox in almost every offensive category, including batting average (.295), runs batted in (84), and runs scored (80). He was also tied for the most homers. *The Sporting News* named him the American League Rookie of the Year.

Chicago manager Al Lopez claimed that Ward, who would post even better power numbers the next season, was one of the main reasons the Sox managed to finish second instead of fifth, as they had in 1962.

No fewer than seventeen to twenty games, Lopez estimated, had been won by the big bat of his prized Canadian rookie.

Ward's father, Jim, was an NHL star during the 1930s. "Driving home three runs with one swing. . . . Bet that hockey-minded dad of mine would call it a hat trick," the younger Ward was quoted as saying after his Opening Day heroics.

Ward's career was cut short by a neck injury and ended in 1970. His lifetime batting average of .254 included 776 hits and 98 home runs.

Big-league baseball comes home to Canada

A gathering of dignitaries on the historic day: (from left) Montreal mayor Jean Drapeau; baseball commissioner Bowie Kuhn; vice chairman of the city of Montreal Gerry Snyder; Quebec premier Jean-Jacques Bertrand; and Expos' president John McHale.

Fans in Montreal — and right across the country — had waited impatiently for this day ever since the announcement two years before that the city had been awarded a National League franchise. Even the thrilling 11–10 season-opening victory over the Mets in New York on April 8 seemed merely a prelude to the historic debut of major-league baseball in Canada.

Throughout Montreal, receptions and parties were held to celebrate the home opener of the Expos. The team had been named for the recent world's fair, which had helped the city land the franchise by giving Montreal so much international exposure.

More than two hundred members of the media were on hand for the game, many of them Americans who had never been to Canada before and who expected to find the field at hastily renovated Jarry Park (a former minor-league facility) covered in snow drifts.

But the day dawned fair and mild, with temperatures reaching 18°C by 1:15 p.m. when Quebec premier Jean-Jacques Bertrand and Montreal mayor Jean Drapeau arrived in a

Dubbed Le Grand Orange, red-haired outfielder Rusty Staub quickly emerged as the darling of the Expo fans and the star of the team.

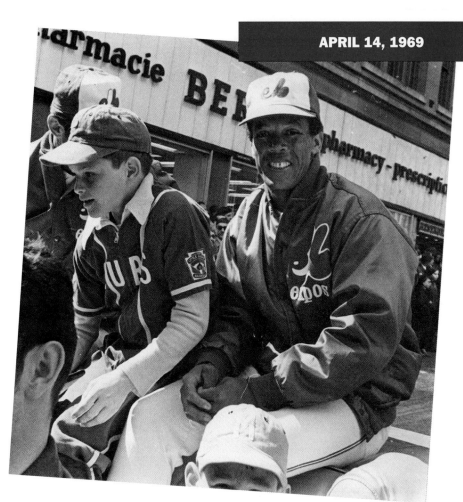

Veteran shortstop Maury Wills was the most famous member of the expansion Expos. Wills stole a record 104 bases in 1962 and was named the National League MVP.

Veteran hurler Jim "Mudcat" Grant greets his new fans during the parade that welcomed the Expos to Montreal. Grant was the starting pitcher for the season opener in New York.

fifteen-car motorcade. The members of the visiting St. Louis Cardinals were introduced, and then the Expos trotted out to a deafening roar of welcome. The fans had already selected their favourites — outfielders Mack Jones and Rusty Staub, pitchers Jim "Mudcat" Grant and Bill Stoneman.

At 1:45 p.m. Premier Bertrand, wearing an Expos' cap, threw out the ceremonial first pitch. Then southpaw Larry Jaster faced down the Cards' leadoff hitter, Lou Brock, and the first big-league game ever played outside the United States was under way.

Every hit, out, and error was cheered as the Expos built a quick 6–0 lead on the strength of a 420-foot, three-run homer by Mack Jones in the first and his two-run triple the following inning. But aided by five Expo errors, St. Louis charged back. The score was tied 7–7 in the seventh when Montreal relief pitcher Dan McGinn singled home the winning run.

A proud city, and an entire country, stood and applauded as Tim McCarver grounded to McGinn for the final out in an 8–7 victory. At long last major-league baseball had come home to Canada.

25

Return of the prodigal son

Once Montreal had been awarded a National League franchise for the 1969 season, most fans assumed that one of the Expos' first priorities would be to make a trade for pitcher Claude Raymond, who was the only French Canadian in the major leagues and was a hero throughout *la belle province*. It was also taken for granted that Raymond would be overjoyed to come home.

So there was considerable surprise when the thirty-two-year-old native of St.-Jean said he wasn't anxious for such a trade — at least not yet. "I just hope they leave me alone one more year," Raymond told reporters during spring-training workouts with the Atlanta Braves. "I know that eventually I'm going to end my career in Montreal and it will be good for me. But this year I want to stay with the Braves and get into the World Series."

Since making his big-league debut with the Chicago White Sox in 1959, Raymond had spent most of his career with also-rans. There was a 3½ year stop in Houston (where he saved sixteen games and was picked for the 1966 All-Star team), as well as two stretches with the Braves. Atlanta was now an emerging powerhouse with a lineup that included sluggers Hank Aaron and Orlando Cepeda.

But Montreal began to look better to Raymond as the season wore on. He was struggling and spent most of his time on the Braves' bench. When word finally came that the Expos had acquired him on waivers, Raymond was ready and even eager for the move, though it did mean leaving a first-place squad for an expansion cellar dweller.

Claude Raymond was a ten-year veteran by the time he came home to Quebec to finish his career. Here he acknowledges the cheers of the crowd during his first game as a Montreal Expo.

When he entered the game, a message of greeting flashed on the scoreboard: "Claude Raymond—Welcome to 'your' park—And long life with the Expos."

He saw action his first night back. The fourteen thousand fans at Jarry Park greeted him with a standing ovation when he entered the game in the eighth inning, with the Expos down 5–1 to San Diego. A message of welcome flashed in French on the outfield scoreboard. The noise level rose with each pitch as he retired the side in order in the only inning he worked.

"In Atlanta I was just a number," said Raymond, who would save a career-high twenty-three games the next season and go on to become an Expos' broadcaster. "But it's different here. It's always nice to have people wanting you and loving you."

Ron Taylor to the rescue

"Once more," photographers kept shouting at Ron Taylor amid the clamour of the New York Mets' dressing room following the second game of the World Series. "Look up, Ron! Smile once more!"

Being a Series hero had become almost routine for Taylor, who

also starred for the St. Louis Cardinals in 1964 when they defeated

Ron Taylor receives congratulations from fellow Mets pitchers Jerry Koosman (in jacket) and Tom Seaver after recording the final out in Game Two of the World Series.

The Toronto native broke in with Cleveland in 1962 and also played for Houston and San Diego during an eleven-year career. He later studied medicine and became the team doctor of the Toronto Blue Jays.

the New York Yankees in seven games. He earned a save in Game Four of that series by pitching four hitless innings at Yankee Stadium. Taylor also appeared in the sixth game, getting the one batter he faced to hit into a double play.

Now he was working his magic for the Miracle Mets, who had astounded the baseball world by rising from the depths of the National League standings to take the pennant and challenge the Baltimore Orioles in the Series. The thirty-one-year-old Toronto native had played a leading role in New York's success, saving thirteen games and winning nine during the regular season, then earning a save and a win against Atlanta in the League Championship Series.

In the World Series opener in Baltimore the day before, Taylor had pitched a flawless two innings in a 4–1 loss to the Orioles. The Mets knew they had to win the second game to keep their hopes alive.

With his team ahead 2–1 in the bottom of the ninth, New York starter Jerry Koosman got the first two outs and then walked Frank Robinson and Boog Powell. Taylor was called in from the bullpen to face the dangerous Brooks Robinson.

He fell behind in the count: ball one, ball two, a curve for a called strike, ball three, an outside pitch that was swung on and missed.

"I was behind Robinson and I was pretty damn worried," said Taylor. His next pitch was an inside sinker that Robinson drilled to the third baseman. The throw beat Robinson to first by two steps.

The Mets never looked back. Taylor's services weren't required again and New York racked up three more wins in succession to take the Series.

In the dressing room after the second game, Taylor was asked if he had come to expect to play the hero's role. Despite owning a perfect 0.00 ERA in 10⅓ innings of relief in playoff and World Series competition, Taylor simply laughed and shook his head.

"When you've had as many line drives hit off you as I have," he answered, "you don't allow yourself to daydream."

John Hiller's miracle comeback

As John Hiller completed his warm-up tosses at Chicago's Comiskey Park, the fans rose out of their seats and offered the opposing pitcher a prolonged ovation. "I don't even remember the first guy I faced," said the Detroit Tigers' twenty-nine-year-old left-hander. "I wasn't excited. I must have been in some sort of a daze, I guess."

Hiller's comeback from the near-fatal heart attack he had suffered eighteen months before was the biggest surprise of the baseball season. Most of the doctors who examined the Toronto native after he'd been stricken felt certain his playing days were over. Yet out there on the mound in Chicago, the once overweight chain-smoker appeared to be in the best shape of his life.

Despite his doctors' prognosis, Hiller had never given up hope of playing again. The biggest hurdle was convincing his physicians and the ballclub that an intensive fitness program had improved his health dramatically. Finally, an eminent heart specialist gave the green light.

In his return at Comiskey, Hiller surrendered four hits in three innings of relief, including a two-run homer to Dick Allen. He appeared twenty-three more times during the regular season, helping the Tigers win their division title. In the League Championship Series against Oakland, he led the pitching staff with three appearances and earned the win in the fourth game.

Even better days were to come. The next season Hiller's record was 10–5 with a miniscule 1.44 ERA. His thirty-eight saves set a new major-league mark and he was named both the Comeback Player of the Year and the Fireman of the Year. In 1974 Hiller's seventeen wins tied the American League mark for most victories by a relief pitcher. By the time Hiller retired in 1980, he had recorded a Detroit club-record 125 saves.

"That guy has more guts than anybody in the clubhouse," said veteran Detroit baseball writer Watson Spoelstra during the summer of Hiller's miracle comeback. "He is an inspiration to the whole team and to everybody everywhere who has ever had heart trouble."

After his return from a massive heart attack, Hiller appeared twenty-four times and saved three games to help the Tigers win their division. The next year the Toronto native was a hero on two counts: his thirty-eight saves set a new major-league record; and in Anaheim, California, he dived into a hotel pool to save a child from drowning.

Reggie Cleveland makes World Series history

There were 56,393 fans crowded into Cincinnati's Riverfront Stadium when Reggie Cleveland became the only Canadian to start a World Series game. The right-hander from Saskatchewan was a model of consistency throughout his career, winning ten games or more seven years in a row.

It was a crucial assignment, unquestionably the most important of his career. But as he walked out to the mound in Cincinnati, Reggie Cleveland had no idea he was about to become the only Canadian pitcher ever to start a World Series game.

"No one told me that until years afterwards," recalled Cleveland, who was born in Swift Current, Saskatchewan. "It was probably just as well. I would have been even more nervous than I already was."

At the age of twenty-seven, the Boston Red Sox right-hander was at the peak of a big-league career that began in 1969 when he broke in with the St. Louis Cardinals. On July 6 his record was 4–6. Then he won nine of his next twelve decisions to help the Red Sox edge Baltimore for their division title.

Boston manager Darrell Johnson gave Cleveland the ball for the second game of the League Championship Series against Oakland, which was the first time a Canadian had started a post-season match. In five innings of work Cleveland surrendered seven hits and departed with the score tied 3–3.

Cleveland appeared three times in the World Series against Cincinnati. A brief but effective relief stint in the third game was followed by his historic start in Game Five.

Pitching against Don Gullett, Cleveland surrendered a run in the fourth on a homer by Tony Perez, and then another run in the fifth. He was knocked out of the game the next inning when Perez homered off him again, this time with two men on. Cincinnati went on to win 6–2 and take a 3–2 lead in the Series.

"I think I just must have been due for a bad game," he said. "I'd been pitching so well for so long."

Boston drew even the next night on Carlton Fisk's dramatic twelfth-inning homer, setting the stage for the decisive seventh game and Cleveland's final appearance.

He got the call with two out and two men on base in the ninth, and the Reds leading 4–3. Johnny Bench walked on a 3-and-2 pitch to load the bases. Then Cleveland ended the threat by getting Perez, his nemesis from Game Five, to fly out.

But the Red Sox were unable to mount a comeback in their half of the inning, and Cincinnati held on to win one of the most thrilling World Series ever played.

The only Canadian to start a Series game went on to record 105 victories during a thirteen-year career, a performance surpassed by only the great Ferguson Jenkins.

"That start in Cincinnati means more to me with every passing year," said Cleveland. "I just wish there had been a happier ending."

St. Louis manager Red Schoendienst welcomes Cleveland to the majors following his debut in 1969. He won forty games for the Cards before being traded to Boston prior to the 1974 season.

33

Sleet and snow can't stop the Blue Jays' debut

The lone Canadian in the Blue Jays' lineup was third baseman Dave McKay, who contributed two singles. McKay later said he "broke out in goose bumps when Anne Murray sang *O Canada*. It was an emotional moment for me . . . if only it had been warmer."

Though snow blanketed the playing field and the thermometer read a bone-chilling −2°C, there was never any serious doubt that the first game in Toronto Blue Jays' history would proceed more or less as scheduled. The capacity crowd of 44,649, all huddled expectantly under fur coats and blankets, had waited too long for this day to take kindly to a postponement. They were already upset about a provincial government decision that prohibited the sale of beer at the ballpark.

And so, as the chant "We Want Beer!" rang out at Exhibition Stadium, singer Anne Murray, dressed in a red parka, slid onto the field to sing *O Canada*. Elaborate opening ceremonies that were to have included Ontario premier Bill Davis (whose government was to blame for the no-beer ruling), Metro chairman Paul Godfrey (the man most responsible for securing the franchise), and baseball commissioner Bowie Kuhn (who had opposed granting Toronto an American League team) were cancelled because of the lousy weather.

At 1:50 p.m. Bill Singer, a sore-armed fourteen-year veteran who had twice won twenty games, threw the first pitch in Blue Jays' history to batter Ralph Garr of the Chicago White Sox. The crowd roared its approval as the umpire thrust out his arm to indicate a strike.

Led by first baseman Doug Ault, who stroked home runs in his first two times at bat, Toronto's collection of expansion cast-offs proceeded to pound fifteen hits off four Chicago pitchers for a 9–5 victory. The lone Canadian in the Blue Jays' lineup, third baseman Dave McKay of Vancouver, contributed two singles.

In the warmth of their new clubhouse the Blue Jays expressed amazement over the enthusiasm of the fans, whose ceaseless cheering had made them want to play despite the cold.

Veteran right-hander Bill Singer gets set to deliver the historic first pitch. By the time he arrived in Toronto, Singer was nearing the end of the line. He appeared in only twelve more games before retiring.

Chicago White Sox player Jack Brohamer adapts to the weather conditions before the game by turning a pair of catcher's leg pads into makeshift skis.

"I love the fans here," said Singer, who left the game in the fifth inning after surrendering four runs. "You could tell they were dying to get major-league baseball in Toronto."

Chicago manager Bob Lemon had a different take on the hardy Torontonians. "How many people were at the park?" he asked a reporter. "Over forty-four thousand? I guess we weren't the only idiots out there."

Terry Puhl bats a playoff record .526

Still the unassuming Canadian kid from the wheat fields of Melville, Saskatchewan, Terry Puhl said he had to pinch himself to believe it was really him leading the Houston challenge against Philadelphia in the National League Championship Series.

"I never, ever thought about anything like this when I was a kid," confessed the twenty-four-year-old Puhl, who stroked ten hits and batted .526, a new record for a five-game playoff series. "All I could think about was playing hockey and cheering for the Maple Leafs."

Three years after being spotted by an Astros' scout at the Canadian midget baseball championships, Puhl was roaming the outfield for the big team. He broke in midway through the 1977 season, then batted .289, .287, and .282 and averaged thirty stolen bases in three full campaigns as a regular. In 1978 he was the lone Astro selected to the All-Star squad.

But because he played in far away Texas, Puhl was unknown to most Canadians until his talents were showcased against Philadelphia in one of the most bitterly contested series in the history of postseason play. Four successive games went into extra innings before a winner was decided.

The Phillies took the opener, but Puhl ignited the Houston offence in the second match by driving home the Astros' first two runs. He also made a sensational catch on a one-hop liner to prevent a Philly score, and his single in the tenth started the winning rally that evened the series.

"That Puhl was unbelievable," said Phillies shortstop Larry Bowa.

Puhl reached base three times as the Astros took the next game, then had an RBI single and stole a base in a 5–3 loss in Game Four. With the series on the line in the fifth game on October 12, he rapped out four hits and scored three times—but

In the National League Championship Series against the Phillies, Puhl did most of his damage at the plate. But he was primarily known for his defensive abilities. The season before, the outfielder had tied a major-league record by playing an entire season without an error.

Always a threat to steal, Puhl swiped two bases in the League Championship Series. His career total of 207 stolen bases is the record for a Canadian-born player.

it wasn't enough. The Phillies advanced to the World Series with an 8–7 triumph in ten innings.

A reporter asked Puhl if he had given any thought to the fact that he was representing Canada.

"Not at all," said the awestruck prairie boy who would go on to play more major-league games than any other Canadian-born ballplayer. "I was too busy thinking of too many other things."

37

Steve Rogers silences his critics

"It's always been said you couldn't win the big one. Were you thinking of that or did you just go out there to try to do the job?"

"Next question, please," snapped Steve Rogers, who had just blanked the Philadelphia Phillies 3–0 on six hits to help the Montreal Expos clinch the first division title in their thirteen-year history. As far as Rogers was concerned, he'd already answered that particular query.

Jubilant teammates pile on Steve Rogers after the final out in Philadelphia.

Steve Rogers reacts after his masterful 3–0 triumph over the Phillies. He answered his critics by scattering six hits and driving in two runs to clinch Montreal's first division title.

Days earlier, catcher Gary Carter had celebrated in his own fashion when Montreal secured a first-place finish in the second half of the season. A seven-week players' strike had divided the campaign into two parts, making the unusual division playoff with Philadelphia necessary.

The once-only division playoff was made necessary by a seven-week players' strike that divided the season in two parts. Philadelphia won the first portion of the interrupted schedule and Montreal took the second half. In the best-of-five showdown with the Phillies, Rogers twice outpitched Steve Carlton, a future hall of famer who had a reputation for *never* losing big games. Rogers had even provided all the offence he would need in the deciding fifth game in Philadelphia, smashing a two-run single in the fifth inning. He allowed just one run in 17⅔ innings of work against the defending World Series champions.

"That man just pitched one of the best games I've ever seen," said Expos shortstop Chris Speier. "There have been so many labels put on him over the years and it's unfair."

Led by young sluggers Gary Carter, Andre Dawson, and Warren Cromartie, the Expos had fallen just short of winning their division the previous two years. In 1979, when Montreal had battled the Pittsburgh Pirates down to the wire, Rogers lost 2–0 to Carlton and the Phillies on the final day of the season. The nine-year veteran had been trying to live down that defeat ever since.

One reason the Expos were able to regroup and win in the second half of the 1981 season was that they replaced their unpopular manager, Dick Williams, with the easygoing Jim Fanning. Another reason for their success was that since the strike, Rogers had gone 7–4 with a miniscule 1.63 ERA.

"I think I've matured," Rogers said after beating Philadelphia. "I think I'm able to separate the emotional part of the game from the physical. When you can do that, I think you eliminate pressure."

Eight days later, in the final game of the League Championship Series against the Los Angeles Dodgers, Rogers surrendered a ninth-inning home run to Rick Monday that would doom the Expos' most promising season — and start all those tired old questions once again.

The All-Star Game goes international

In keeping with the international flavour of the 53rd All-Star Game, baseball commissioner Bowie Kuhn even tried speaking French during the gala pre-game luncheon. "Magnifique hospitalité . . . impeccable," Kuhn commended everyone in Montreal who had helped organize the game — the first ever played outside of the United States.

Canadian prime minister Pierre Trudeau was up next and he stole the show with a series of one-liners. Trudeau said his late father, who had once been vice-president of the International League Montreal Royals, would have been proud that his son was addressing such an august gathering of baseball greats, but he would have preferred to see him there as a player.

"Certainly if he took a look at the lineup of both head tables, he would realize that I would be the lowest paid here — and I don't have an option clause in my contract." Trudeau concluded his speech by noting that most Canadians were Expo fans. "The rest of them go around lighting candles for the Blue Jays."

As with almost every mid-season classic, most of the fun was provided by the hoopla surrounding the game. In a special Salute

Prime Minister Pierre Trudeau is flanked by baseball commissioner Bowie Kuhn (left) and former commissioner A. B. "Happy" Chandler. Trudeau is said to have encouraged Kuhn to consider Vancouver as a future site for a big-league franchise.

Five members of a powerful Montreal Expos' squad were named to the National League lineup: (from left) Gary Carter, Andre Dawson, Steve Rogers, Tim Raines, and Al Oliver.

The elaborate opening ceremonies included a special Salute to International Baseball. Twelve former baseball greats from around the world simultaneously made the ceremonial first pitch.

to International Baseball, former big-league stars representing eleven different countries were called upon to jointly throw out the ceremonial first pitch. Canada's delegates were Quebec native Claude Raymond and 1930s Yankee star George Selkirk, who was born in Huntsville, Ontario.

The powerful Expos' squad had five members in the National League lineup, including the starting pitcher, Steve Rogers. Local hero Gary Carter received a tremendous ovation from Olympic Stadium's capacity crowd of 59,057 when he was introduced as the top vote-getter in All-Star balloting.

The game itself produced few surprises. The Nationals won 4–1, giving the senior circuit its eleventh straight victory and nineteenth in the last twenty games. Cincinnati shortstop Dave Concepcion was named the MVP on the strength of a two-run homer and his superb play in the field.

Fortunately, whenever the action lagged, fans could direct their attention to Prime Minister Trudeau, who through the night amazed everyone with his uncanny ability to catch tossed peanuts in his mouth.

Jays subdue Yanks for first division title

From one day to the next the banner headlines on a Toronto daily changed from "Heartbreak!" to "At Last!"

Down to the final three games in a season-long battle with the New York Yankees for first place, the Blue Jays returned home to Exhibition Stadium and a weekend showdown with their red-hot rivals. The Yanks could force a playoff by sweeping the series. On Friday night, in the opener, the single win Toronto needed to clinch the first division title in the franchise's nine-year history appeared to be firmly within their grasp. But with a 3–2 lead and two away in the ninth inning, Yankee Butch Wynegar homered to tie the score. Moments later, Jay centre fielder Lloyd Moseby muffed a routine fly ball, which allowed the winning run to cross the plate.

By the start of the next afternoon's game, the tension was almost unendurable for the faithful who filled the stadium. Mercifully, the outcome was never in doubt. Veteran right-hander Doyle Alexander limited the New Yorkers to five hits, leading the Jays to a 5–1 victory. Ernie Whitt, Willie Upshaw, and Moseby, who had been disconsolate after his error, all contributed home runs.

Left fielder George Bell made the final putout, circling under a softly arcing fly ball as thousands held their breath. Bell made the grab and then dropped to his knees, his face suffused with joy.

The chant "We're Number One!" went up as many fans stormed the field. Alexander was raised on the shoulders of his teammates and carried to the clubhouse for a champagne shower. Outside the crowd lingered, reluctant to let the moment go.

"This is a momentous occasion," one teenager said as he scooped infield dirt into a cup. "This is history right here, the Jays' first championship. Now we [have] to win the World Series."

A comeback victory by the Kansas City Royals in the League Championship Series would put that dream on hold for several years. But for a while longer at the stadium, and on through the night in the streets of downtown Toronto, the Jays' first victory party would carry on unabated.

Outfielder George Bell goes down on his knees after making the final putout in Toronto's division-clinching victory over the New York Yankees.

Opposite:
The hero of the day was pitcher Doyle Alexander, who surrendered only five hits in leading the Jays to a 5–1 win. The thirty-five-year-old Alexander had earlier been cast aside by the Yankees, who were still paying all but $60,000 of his $800,000 annual salary.

Ernie Whitt leads record homer barrage

44

Canadian rookie Rob Ducey contributed the record-tying eighth home run of the game, which was also the first of his big-league career. Ducey was the third Canadian to play for the Blue Jays, following infielder Dave McKay of Vancouver and outfielder Paul Hodgson of Fredericton, New Brunswick.

Opposite:
Ernie Whitt acknowledges the cheers of the crowd after hitting his third home run in Toronto's 18–3 mauling of the Baltimore Orioles. Whitt's final blast was the ninth homer of the night for the Jays, who became the first team ever to hit more than eight in a game.

"The way we threw the ball up to the plate, they couldn't help but hit it," said a disgusted Cal Ripken Sr., the Baltimore Orioles' manager. Over in the Toronto clubhouse, the Blue Jays celebrated their record ten home runs with raucous jokes about the need to move the outfield fences back, and about how there would now be cries throughout the league of "Break up the Blue Jays!"

Ernie Whitt led history's greatest single game home-run assault by hitting three; George Bell and Rance Mulliniks contributed two apiece; and Lloyd Moseby, Fred McGriff, and Canadian rookie Rob Ducey chipped in with solo shots. Before a thrilled evening crowd of 27,446 at Toronto's Exhibition Stadium, the Blue Jays shattered the old major-league team homer mark of eight (achieved seven times before) as they romped to an 18–3 victory over the Orioles.

"There's no question I was going up there thinking home run," Whitt said of his final round-tripper, a three-run blast that sailed over the right-field fence in the seventh inning. "It's not often you have a chance to set a major-league record. When the count got to 3-and-1, I was looking for a pitch and I got it."

The popular catcher was given a prolonged ovation as he rounded the bases, then was called out of the dugout to take a final bow. Otto Velez was the only other Blue Jay who had ever hit three homers in one game.

One inning later McGriff brought the final tally to ten with a leadoff shot into the stands in right-centre. McGriff's homer was his nineteenth of the season, surpassing the old Blue Jay rookie mark of eighteen set by Jesse Barfield in 1982.

Perhaps the most excited Blue Jay was Rob Ducey, whose home run in the seventh — the record-tying eighth of the game — was the first of his big-league career. Manager Jimy Williams had inserted the twenty-two-year-old native of Cambridge, Ontario, into the lineup late in the game in place of centre fielder Lloyd Moseby.

"I'm glad I got it tonight," Ducey said. "What will stick in my mind most is the major-league record. We'll be in Cooperstown now."

45

SkyDome opens to mixed reviews

Built at a cost of approximately $500 million, Toronto's SkyDome was, depending on your point of view, either a spectacular success that would forever redefine the nature of ballparks, or an abysmal, impersonal failure, better suited to tractor pulls than the playing of the grand old game.

"The heck with old parks like Comiskey and Fenway," gushed reliever Mark Knudson of the visiting Milwaukee Brewers, the Blue Jays' opponents in the SkyDome opener. "They've outlived their usefulness."

"It looks like B.C. Place with a toupee," cracked Vancouver *Sun* columnist Pete McMartin, referring to his city's bubble-like covered stadium.

On June 5 a capacity crowd of 48,378 rubbernecking fans turned out to see for themselves. Judging by their prolonged cheers when the pre-game ceremonies began shortly before 7:30 p.m., SkyDome was a success.

The players were introduced, then Toronto starter Jimmy Key trotted to the mound to begin the game. Key's historic first pitch was a strike that Milwaukee leadoff man Paul Molitor took looking. Two pitches later Molitor had the first hit in the new stadium, a double past shortstop Tony Fernandez. Molitor then became the first runner to step across home plate when he scored on Gary Sheffield's grounder.

It was not the Jays' night. Toronto left eight men stranded on base in a 5–3 defeat. Afterwards, the Jays expressed their delight with SkyDome, although there was some concern that their home-run output might diminish in their spacious new home. Jay Fred McGriff had hit the stadium's first homer in the second inning, but several other drives that definitely would have gone out of old Exhibition Stadium were hauled down at the warning track.

The most frustrating of these was a long blast by pinch hitter Bob Brenly in the eighth that could have got the Jays back in the game. "Well," Brenly deadpanned to reporters, "I never have had any luck hitting in this park."

This aerial view of SkyDome during the Jays' home opener was taken from a window washer's cage on the CN Tower.

Opposite:
Awestruck members of the Toronto Blue Jays survey their new $500 million home before the start of the opener against Milwaukee. For Toronto fans the night was slightly tainted by a 5–3 Blue Jay loss.

Fergie Jenkins joins the game's immortals

Dozens of Maple Leaf flags waved proudly in the air and a band from his home town of Chatham, Ontario, played "Canadian Sunset" as Ferguson Arthur Jenkins stepped forward to become Canada's first member of the Baseball Hall of Fame.

"I want to thank the city of Chatham," began Jenkins' address to the overflow crowd in Cooperstown, New York. "And to my first country, Canada, the nation where I was born, I owe a great deal. My love for Canada is immeasurable."

Jenkins had earned his place among the pantheon by compiling a record of 284 wins and 226 losses during a nineteen-year career with the Philadelphia Phillies, Chicago Cubs, Texas Rangers, and Boston Red Sox. From 1967 to 1972 he recorded six consecutive twenty-win seasons for the Cubs. Jenkins received the Cy Young Award in 1971.

For every ballplayer fortunate enough to be elected, induction into the Hall of Fame is the pinnacle of his career. But for Jenkins, the celebration was tainted by tragedy. In January, just four days after he had learned of his selection, his wife, Maryanne, died of

Canada's greatest ballplayer paused several times to fight back tears during his acceptance speech at Cooperstown. Hundreds of proud Canadian fans were on hand for the ceremony, including Derek Burney, the Canadian ambassador to the United States.

Jenkins, winner of the 1971 Cy Young Award as the National League's top hurler, demonstrates the pitching form that enabled him to record 284 victories during a nineteen-year career.

Opposite:
Jenkins posed with fellow inductees Rod Carew (left) and Gaylord Perry (centre). Baseball greats Joe DiMaggio, Ted Williams, Willie Mays, Juan Marichal, and Enos Slaughter also attended the ceremony in Cooperstown.

injuries sustained in an automobile accident. Jenkins made reference to her death in his speech, stopping several times to compose himself.

"The fabric of life is interwoven with wins, with losses, with successes, joys, and tragedies," he said. "We cannot know the pattern of the fabric of life. But we can try to understand the mystery that it holds."

Fellow pitcher Gaylord Perry and batting star Rod Carew were inducted into the hall with Jenkins, but it was clear that many in the audience were there expressly to see the Canadian honoured. At least six hundred old friends and neighbours came by bus from Chatham, and many more fans arrived from across Canada.

Jenkins concluded by thanking his mother, dead for more than twenty years, and his eighty-four-year-old father, seated in a wheelchair in the front row, who had played in the old Negro Leagues before the integration of baseball.

Hugging his induction plaque to his chest, Canada's greatest ballplayer paused as his countrymen waved their flags and the crowd rose to its feet. "I have your love," Jenkins said, his voice holding steady. "Thank you very much."

49

Dennis Martinez is pitcher perfect

Montreal Expo Dennis Martinez had two countries celebrating right along with him after he became only the fifteenth pitcher in baseball history to retire twenty-seven consecutive batters for a perfect game.

In his native Nicaragua, where the thirty-six-year-old right-hander was a national hero known as El Presidente, there were fireworks and dancing in the streets when news came of his 2–0 shutdown of the Dodgers in Los Angeles. And back in Canada, Expo officials placed a rush order for twenty-five thousand copies of a commemorative poster, to be ready in time for the team's return four days later.

"This game was for God, myself, my family, the people of Nicaragua, and the Expos," a tearful Martinez said. His perfect game was the first in Expos' history (to go along with six no-hitters) and the first in the majors since 1988.

Martinez, who said he was thinking no-hitter "from the first hitter to the last," threw just ninety-five pitches (sixty-five of them for strikes) and struck out five Dodgers. In raising his season's record to 11–6, he was forced to a 3-and-2 count on only three hitters.

But there had been a couple of close calls along the way. In the fourth, Canadian Larry Walker, who was filling in for Gold Glove winner Andres Galarraga at first base, blocked a bouncing drive with his right forearm. Walker recovered the ball and threw just in time to Martinez covering at first.

Three innings later Dodger Juan Samuel dropped down a bunt that sent Martinez sprawling to the ground before he came up with the ball and fired to Walker for the out.

It was Walker who drove in the winning run in the seventh, when he slashed a Mike Morgan pitch to the centre-field wall for a triple. Walker then scored on a grounder by catcher Ron Hassey,

Dennis Martinez waves to the Dodger Stadium crowd after tossing the first perfect game in Expos' history. No one had ever no-hit the Dodgers at home in the thirty-year history of the stadium.

50

Third baseman Tim Wallach (left) and Canadian Larry Walker, who drove home the winning run, rush in to celebrate with Martinez after the final out. Martinez's record now stood at 174–140 in fifteen big-league seasons.

who was also behind the plate for the perfect game thrown by Cleveland's Len Barker in 1981 and is the only backstop in history to catch two perfect games.

Martinez told reporters he was in a daze after recording the final out. "I didn't know what to think, what to say. I thought I was dreaming," said the fifteen-year veteran, who from that point on would be known in both Nicaragua and Canada as El Perfecto.

A miracle on grass for Canadian teens

Any optimism surrounding Canada's chances in the World Youth Baseball Championship had all but dissipated after the national team lost an exhibition match to the Netherlands, a nation not exactly known as a baseball power. Canada had finished fifth the previous three years, and most observers felt they'd be lucky to climb that high in the standings again.

And yet, when the infield dust had settled at a packed West-bran Stadium in Brandon, Manitoba, Canada's best sixteen-to eighteen-year-old ballplayers had produced an upset that was immediately dubbed the Miracle on Grass. "I'm so glad we're number one. . . . It's a tremendous feeling," said star pitcher Daniel Brabant of Longueuil, Quebec, who led the way to a 5–2 victory over Chinese Taipei (Taiwan) in the final game as Canada captured its first championship in the eleven-year history of the tournament. The best finishes Canada had previously managed were thirds in 1983 and 1987.

The young Canadians fashioned their victory on solid defence and the superlative pitching of Brabant, the winner of three games in as many starts. Brabant, whose ERA was 0.46 for the tourney, hurled a four-hitter through 5⅔ innings in the final before an arm injury forced him to leave the game. Shortstop Todd Betts of Toronto drove in three runs to pace the attack.

A key factor in Canada's triumph was its earlier 10–6 come-back win over a highly regarded U.S. squad. Canada and the United States finished the round-robin portion of the tournament with identical 7–2 records, but Canada gained entry into the final against first-place Chinese Taipei (who had defeated Canada in their previous encounter) on the strength of its victory over the Americans.

Many who were on hand in Brandon called the victory a coming-of-age for baseball in this country.

"If the country nurtures these kids and lets them become better players day by day, there is no doubt in my mind that many of these young men can have tremendous futures in the game," said John Haar, Canada's head coach. "There is no other way to put it. This is our future."

Members of the Canadian squad pose for a group shot after delivering their country's first championship in the eleven-year history of the tournament. Canada had never finished better than third.

Outfielder Kevin Collins doffs his cap to the crowd after accepting his gold medal from Brandon mayor Rick Borotsik.

Canada's Todd Betts argues a called third strike during a game earlier in the tournament. A crucial victory over the United States gave Canada its berth in the final.

Star Canadian hurler Daniel Brabant holds his injured shoulder as he is escorted from the mound in the final game against Chinese Taipei. Brabant won three games in the tourney.

53

Blue Jays bring home a championship at last

So often in years past the Toronto Blue Jays had broken the hearts of fans across the country by not being quite good enough, or determined enough, when it counted most. But Dave Winfield, Joe Carter, Robbie Alomar, and the others who faced the persistent Atlanta Braves in the crucial sixth game of the World Series were determined to prove they were made of better stuff than their predecessors.

Even when the Braves came back to tie it 2–2 in the ninth inning there was no panic, no thought of defeat. "I thought, 'Okay I've got a blown save, big deal,'" said reliever Tom Henke, who had been just one out away from delivering Canada's first World Series championship. "It's a tied game and that don't mean nothing. Time to bear down and keep it that way."

The deadlock in Atlanta continued into the top of the eleventh. Toronto's Devon White and Robbie Alomar stood on base with two out. To the plate stepped Dave Winfield, whose brilliant twenty-year career seemed to have led inevitably to this defining moment.

Winfield, slumping to this point in the Series, drove a Charlie Leibrandt changeup past Atlanta's third baseman to score both runners. The Braves got one run back in their half of the inning. Then, with two out, Otis Nixon, whose single had tied it in the ninth, dropped a bunt that Jays pitcher Mike Timlin fielded cleanly. Timlin set himself, then tossed the ball to Carter at first to beat the fleet Nixon by a full step.

At that moment Canadians joined in the biggest national celebration since Team Canada's Paul Henderson defeated the Soviets in 1972 by scoring hockey's most famous goal. Street parties broke out spontaneously in towns and cities across the country, while in Toronto a half-million revellers blocked traffic in the downtown core.

Thousands showed their devotion to the new World Series champions by jamming the streets of downtown Toronto during the victory parade. "This is a team of players from America and Latin America, but we still feel the pride of Canada," said pitcher David Cone, who waved a Maple Leaf flag at the crowd.

Dave Winfield strokes one of the most crucial hits in Blue Jays' history — a two-run, eleventh-inning double down the third base line that lifted the Jays to their first World Series title.

"I'm turning inside with joy and happiness for all of us in this room, in this organization," Jays manager Cito Gaston shouted over the bedlam in the dressing room. "We've been trying a long time for this."

An entire country had been waiting just as long — and just as impatiently.

"This one's for Canada, for all the people," saluted Tom Henke, tipping a bottle of champagne to his lips.

Montreal's Canadian trio

Larry Walker, Maple Ridge, British Columbia.

 There was never any question that Denis Boucher was the star attraction. The homecoming of the twenty-five-year-old southpaw from Lachine, Quebec, had been long-anticipated. A Labour Day crowd of 40,066 fans, the largest since Opening Day, showed up at Olympic Stadium to cheer him on. Before the start of the game, the Expo team mascot draped a provincial flag over the pitcher's mound, and by the time Boucher had set down the Colorado Rockies on five pitches in the first inning, he had already received four standing ovations.

Almost overlooked in all the excitement surrounding the debut of Boucher—who followed reliever Claude Raymond as only the second Quebec-born player in Expos' history—was that for the first time ever, three Canadians were in the starting lineup of a big-league club.

"It was really an exciting day for everyone here and for Canada in general," said Boucher's batterymate, Joe Siddall of Windsor, Ontario. Siddall and right fielder Larry Walker of Maple Ridge, British Columbia, comprised the other two-thirds of the Canadian contingent.

All three native sons played leading roles in Montreal's 4–3 victory, with Walker slamming a solo homer, Siddall doubling home a run, and Boucher contributing six innings of six-hit ball before leaving the game with a 2–1 lead. He lost his opportunity to record the win when the Rockies briefly came back to tie the score in the seventh.

Denis Boucher, Lachine, Quebec.

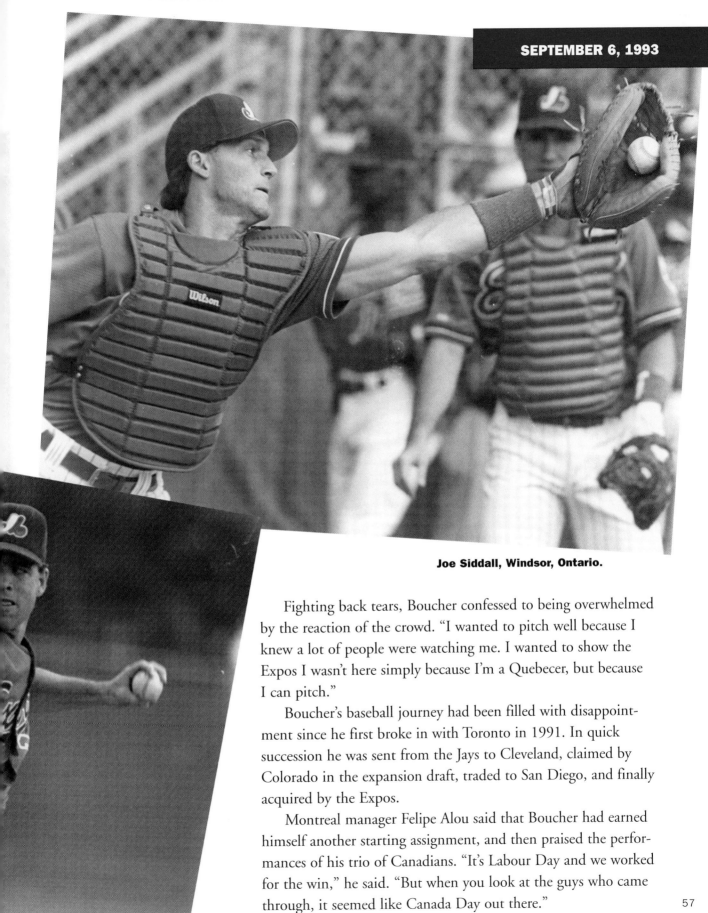

Joe Siddall, Windsor, Ontario.

Fighting back tears, Boucher confessed to being overwhelmed by the reaction of the crowd. "I wanted to pitch well because I knew a lot of people were watching me. I wanted to show the Expos I wasn't here simply because I'm a Quebecer, but because I can pitch."

Boucher's baseball journey had been filled with disappointment since he first broke in with Toronto in 1991. In quick succession he was sent from the Jays to Cleveland, claimed by Colorado in the expansion draft, traded to San Diego, and finally acquired by the Expos.

Montreal manager Felipe Alou said that Boucher had earned himself another starting assignment, and then praised the performances of his trio of Canadians. "It's Labour Day and we worked for the win," he said. "But when you look at the guys who came through, it seemed like Canada Day out there."

57

Jays' Joltin' Joe makes it two in a row

Joe Carter joyously leaps around the bases following his historic Series-winning home run. With his blast, the Jays became the first back-to-back champions since the New York Yankees in 1977 and 1978.

Before the start of the season, Joe Carter said that God had come to him in a dream and told him to re-sign with the Toronto Blue Jays.

Along with millions of Canadians, perhaps even the Almighty was shouting and jumping with joy when Carter's ninth-inning blast delivered the Jays into the promised land of back-to-back World Series championships. "This is absolute paradise," an elated Carter said after he had leapt around the bases and been carried off the field by his teammates. "It's the situation you dream about when you're a kid. I still can't believe it went out."

Toronto's six-game triumph over the Philadelphia Phillies made them the first team in fifteen years to win consecutive titles. They'd done it in large part by spending their riches to re-sign Carter and acquire slugger Paul Molitor to replace departed fan-favourite Dave Winfield. Though he was brilliant all season long,

Series MVP Paul Molitor delivers the single that put him on first base when Joe Carter came to the plate in the ninth. Molitor hit an even .500 for the Series, with eight runs batted in.

Torontonian Rob Butler was the first Canadian to appear in a World Series since Reggie Cleveland pitched for the Boston Red Sox in 1975. The Blue Jay outfielder contributed a pinch-hit single in Game Five in Philadelphia.

Molitor was even better in the World Series. The sixteen-year veteran hit an even .500 with eight runs batted in and was named the Series MVP.

In the deciding game at Toronto's SkyDome, Molitor tripled and homered in the early going. Then, with one out in the bottom of the ninth, his sinking liner to centre field placed him on first as Carter walked to the plate. The Phils led 6–5. Rickey Henderson, who had walked, was on second. And on the mound was Mitch "Wild Thing" Williams, a closer who lived up to his nickname too often for the comfort of Philly fans and whose presence now gave hope to the Toronto faithful.

Carter worked the count to 2-and-2. Then Williams delivered a slider down low, right where the Blue Jay liked them. "I was hunched down a little and I kind of lost it in the lights," Carter recounted. "I looked up and saw it had a tail on it. Then everything went into slow motion."

His was the first Series-winning homer since the Pirates' Bill Mazeroski defeated the Yankees in 1960. And just as Carter had known he was meant to re-sign with Toronto, he told reporters he had also had a hunch that something special was going to happen that night. "But I'll be danged!" he said. "I never quite expected that."

The champions who might have been

One local radio station started a futile petition to have the Montreal Expos declared baseball's official champions, and there was even talk of staging a mock World Series against the New York Yankees, who had finished atop the American League standings.

No one in Montreal seemed willing to let the dream die. When the players went out on strike in mid-August, the Expos' record of 74–40 was the best in the major leagues. Montreal enjoyed a six-game cushion over second-place Atlanta in the National League Eastern Division, and the team's first appearance in postseason play since 1981 seemed certain.

Though handicapped by one of the lowest payrolls in baseball, the Expos had built a young, talented, and always exciting lineup. The pitching staff was led by starter Ken Hill, who had been heading towards a twenty-win season. Budding superstar Moises Alou topped the team with a .339 batting average. And Canadian Larry Walker, the Expos' highest-paid performer at $4.025 million per season, was having perhaps his best season yet, with nineteen homers, eighty-six runs batted in, and a batting average of .322.

The walk-out lasted thirty-four days before baseball's acting commissioner, Bud Selig, officially declared the season dead on September 14. Plans for a drastic overhaul of the game's economic structure, starting with the implementation of a salary cap, were rejected by the players. Despite the hopeful suggestions of Expo boosters, for the first time since 1904 no World Series of any kind would be played.

Montreal team officials estimated the season's premature end would cost the already financially beleaguered franchise as much as $20 million in lost revenue. What hurt even more was missing out on the chance to bring home the first championship in the twenty-six-year history of the team.

"We had the players to win and we had the best record in baseball," said Expos general manager Kevin Malone. "I thought we were getting better every day. It's a shame we didn't have the chance to finish what we had started."

But perhaps manager Felipe Alou said it best for every heart-broken Montreal fan, player, and team official. "I feel like the fisherman who has made a record catch, but has to throw the fish back."

The Expos of 1994 were a young and exciting squad that many felt had the talent to be World Series champions. They finished the strike-shortened season with the best record in baseball.

Acknowledgements

I would like to thank the following for their generosity and support: Jim Shearon, author of *Canada's Baseball Legends*; Canadian baseball historian and author Bill Humber; Ray McNeil of the Canadian Baseball Hall of Fame; Monique Giroux of the Montreal Expos; Howard Starkman and Bonnie Way of the Toronto Blue Jays; and Sharon McAuley, my wife and baseball companion.

Photo Credits

Sandy Black: 52 (*top*); *Brandon Sun*/Pam Doyle: 53 (*both*), Desmond Murray: 52–53; Canadian Baseball Hall of Fame: 8, 18, 28, 29, 36, 37, 48 (*top*); Canapress: 39 (*top*); Canada Wide — Bill Sandford: 44, Fred Thornhill: 47, Mark O'Neill: 54, Stan Behal: 55, Mike Cassese: 59; Hockey Hall of Fame: 23 (*top*); Phil Marchildon private collection: 21 (*both*); Montreal Expos: 24 (*both*), 25 (*both*), 26, 27, 38, 39 (*bottom*), 40, 41 (*both*), 50, 51, 56 (*top*), 56–57, 57 (*top*), 60 (*top*), 60–61; National Archives of Canada: 10; National Baseball Library and Archive, Cooperstown, New York: 9, 11, 12, 13, 14, 15, 16, 17, 19, 20, 22, 23 (*bottom*), 31, 32, 48 (*bottom*), 49; Toronto Blue Jays: 34 (*top*), 45, 59 (*bottom*); *Toronto Star* — 33; Graham Bezant: 34 (*bottom*), Boris Spremo: 35, Colin McConnell: 42, Tony Bock: 43, Mike Slaughter: 46, Jeff Goode: 58.

Index